Mel Bay Presents... # HOW TO PLAY BLUES & BOOGIE

by Paul T. Smith

© 1982 BY MEL BAY PUBLICATIONS, INC. PACIFIC, MO.
INTERNATIONAL COPYRIGHT SECURED. ALL RIGHTS RESERVED. PRINTED IN U.S.A.

CONTENTS

About the Author	3
The Blues	4
Bass Lines and Chord Lines	5
Blues Bass Lines	6
Blues Chords	7
Modern Blues Bass Lines	9
Substitute Chords	11
Basic Blues Type Choruses	14
More Advanced Blues	18
About Blues Jazz Exercises 1-A through 4-A	22
Blues Jazz Ex. 1-A	23
Blues Jazz Ex. 2-A	24
Blues Jazz Ex. 3-A	25
Blues Jazz Ex. 4-A	26
4/4 and 6/8 Blues	27
About the Sixth Way and 4ths and 5ths Blues	30
The Sixth Way	31
4ths and 5ths Blues	32
Boogie Woogie	33
Boogie Woogie Bass Lines	34
Boogie Woogie	35
More Bass Figures	37
Right Hand Figures	39
Short Boogie	44
Minor Boogie	47
Mel's Boogie	51
Other Books and Records by the Author	55

ABOUT THE AUTHOR — PAUL T. SMITH

... Joined Johnny Richards band in 1941 as pianist-arranger.
... Joined Ozzie Nelson's band in 1942, also arranger for the Red Skelton Radio show at that time.
... Played with the Les Paul trio and the Andrews Sisters in '46 and early '47.
... Joined Tommy Dorsey Orchestra as pianist-arranger in 1947 through 1948.
... Became rehearsal pianist at Warner Bros. studio in 1949.
... Was NBC staff pianist in Hollywood from 1950 through 1962.
... Recorded extensively with Billy May, Paul Weston, Les Baxter, Ray Anthony, and other big bands during the '50s.
... Was an Arranger-Composer on many industrial films and commercials.
... Was the Accompanist for almost every singer who appeared on NBC in Hollywood between 1950 and 1962.
... Pianist-Conductor for Ella Fitzgerald, Sammy Davis, Jr., Pat Boone, Steve Allen TV show, Rosemary Clooney, Edie Adams, Joni James, Bing Crosby and others.
... Has approximately 50 solo albums on Capitol, Verve, MGM, Imperial, Warner Bros., Discwasher and currently recording extensively on Outstanding Records, an independent company based in Huntington Beach, Calif. At this writing, there are 10 albums available on the Outstanding Label.
... Was a studio musician from 1950 through 1981 and is still at it.
... Is currently playing at the Velvet Turtle in Redondo Beach, California with his duo, teaching and doing studio work.

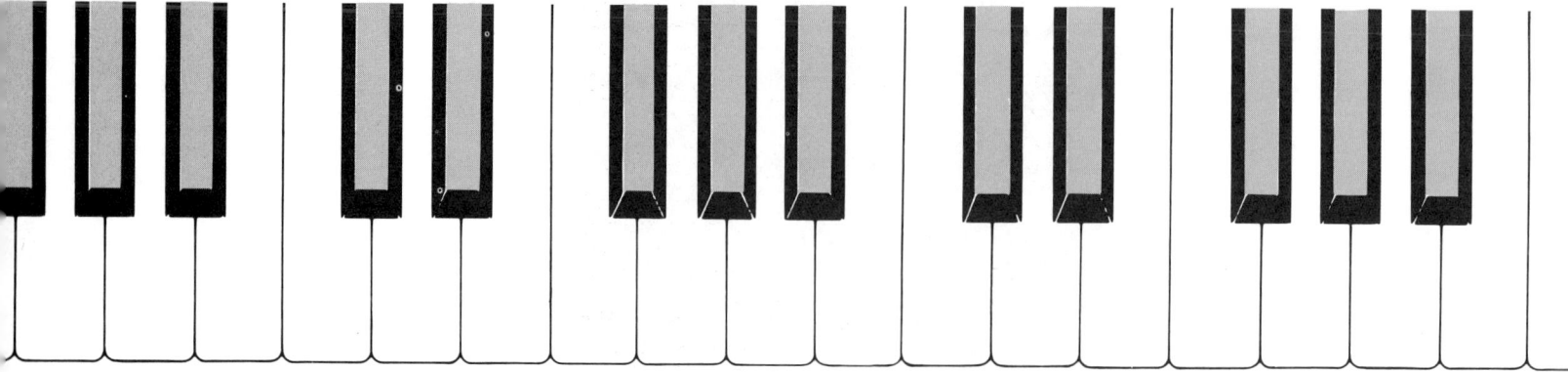

THE BLUES

The blues is the simplest form of American jazz. The basic chord structure is extremely simple and does not require any harmonic knowledge. The blues chord progressions have been the basic source of improvising for years, especially by the self-taught players who have not had any training in harmony and harmonic changes.

The basic blues have only 4 chords in a 12-bar phrase. Throughout the years the four chords have been enlarged upon so as to make the harmonic changes more interesting.

Throughout the book, I will give you a series of different chord changes based on the blues so that you won't have to be bored with the original 4 chords. Later we will deal with several boogie bass lines that are standard in playing this kind of music.

I will give you a few examples with just a lead-line and the chords (with chord symbols). The first few pages are the absolute simple, beginning bass lines and chords for playing the basic blues. They are not necessarily traditional, but they are simple and to the point. As we progress, I'll give examples of more progressive blues progressions and a few funky figures that can be used to make your blues sound reasonably modernized.

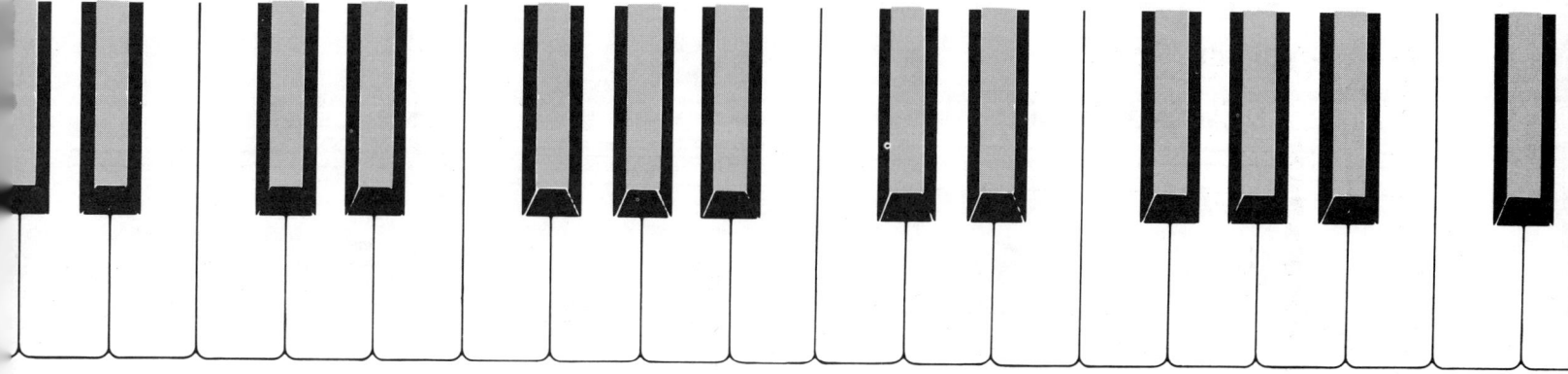

BASS LINES AND CHORD LINES

The following pages are devoted to the basic, down-home bass lines and chord structures which are the foundation of the blues. If improvising comes reasonably easy to you, then, by all means, add a bluesy melody line to the simplified bass and chord lines. If improvising is not easy for you, then just get the basic chords and bass lines down so you play them easily. Then try to pick out a blues-oriented progression of notes to fit the lines.

Blues Bass Lines

BLUES CHORDS

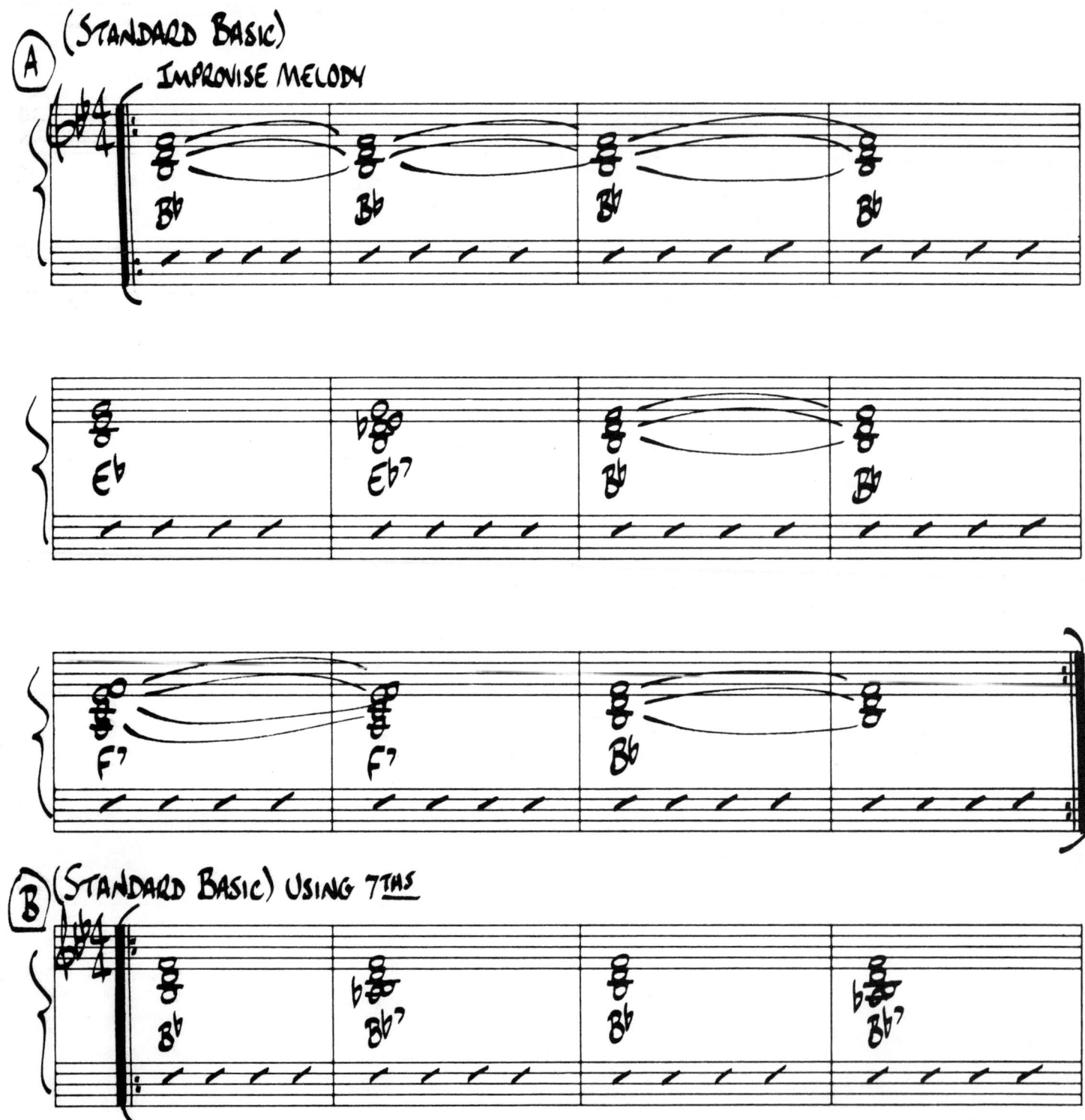

Modern Blues Bass Lines

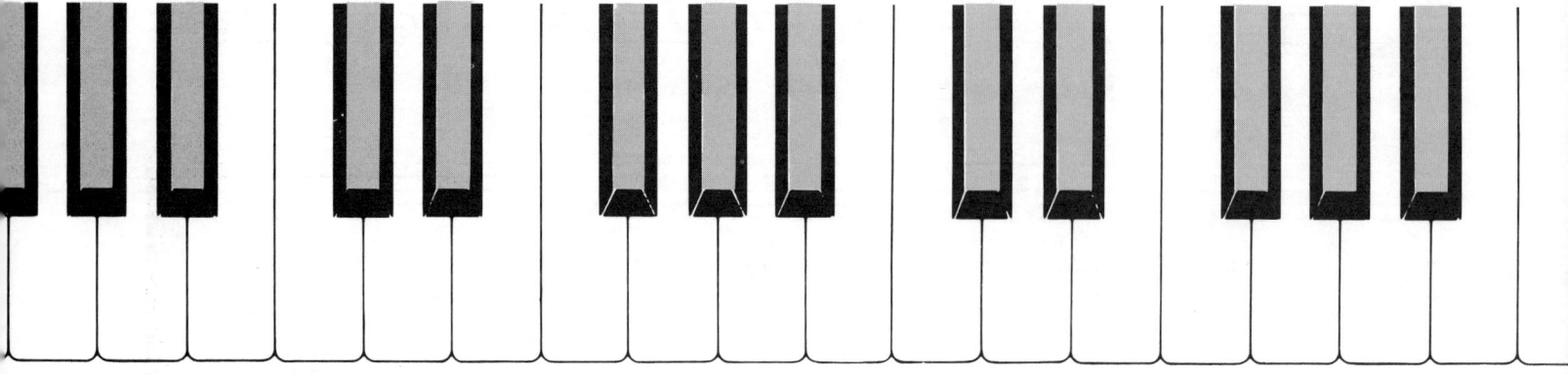

SUBSTITUTE CHORDS

Since the blues chords are so simple, it is necessary to find a few other chord progressions that will substitute for the "vanilla" chords used in the basic blues. The monotony of the 3 or 4 basic chords can be relieved by adding a few more changes of our own. Experiment on your own and see if you can find some interesting chord changes that will alternate with the basic ones.

SUBSTITUTE CHORDS

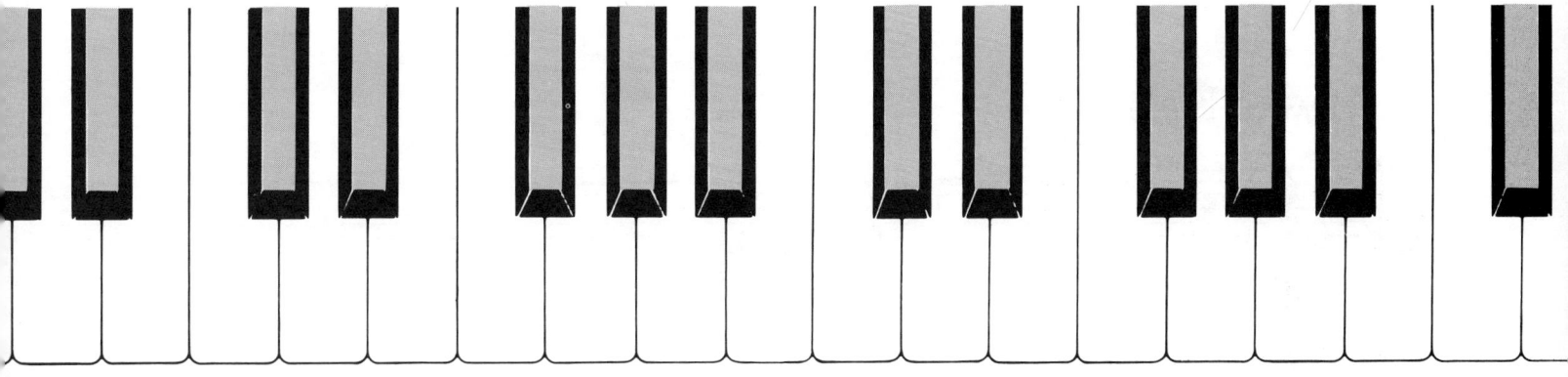

BASIC BLUES TYPE CHORUSES

The following three 12-bar choruses are just examples of the type of bluesy melodies you can concoct to fit the chords. They are all to be played lazily, not percussively. (All of which is typical of slower blues).

Basic Blues Type Choruses

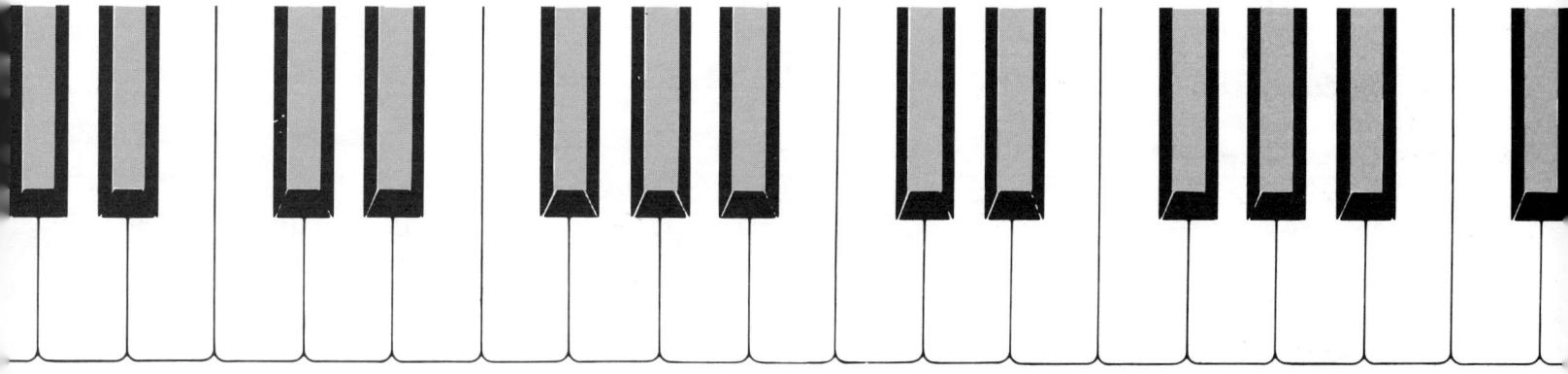

MORE ADVANCED BLUES

Here are some blues choruses utilizing the 3rds and 4ths that are possible against given chords. The first two are at slow to medium tempos. Again, they are not to be played loudly, percussively or with too much enthusiasm. The figures swing by themselves, so it isn't necessary to push to "TRY" to make them swing. The 3rd chorus (C) is in the style of the late Errol Garner, and the left hand has that chunky pulsation which was Errol's stock and trade. This is also not to be played too loudly, rather just quietly swinging. You may find that you can play the bottom note of the left hand chord just a slight bit ahead of the rest of the chord, which gets a kind of rolling rhythm going in the left hand. Kind of a "ker-chunk" feeling instead of the straight-up-and-down feeling of "chunk chunk Chunk". How about that for a description of rhythm!!!

More Advanced Blues

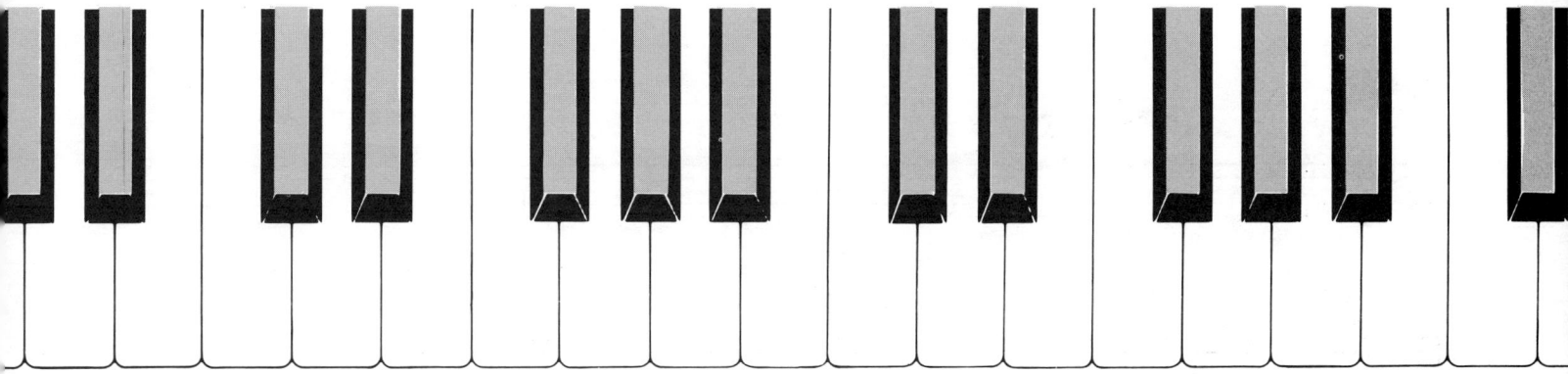

BLUES JAZZ EX. 1A

On the following Jazz exercises, you may add whatever you feel to the exercises. 1A is pretty much self-contained, however you may feel that you wish to add something to the left hand. If it is played loosely and relaxed, it will play pretty well just as is.

BLUES JAZZ EX. 2A, 3A, and 4A

These may be used as double hand exercises if you wish or you may comp with the left hand plunking the chords and play the figures as written with the right hand. Make sure you play the right hand figures as straight 8ths, not like dotted 8ths and 16ths. As you progress with this idea, you will find yourself accenting certain notes (your choice) and thus making the figures sound less like Mozart and more "hip".

Blues Jazz Ex. 1-A

Blues Jazz Ex. 2-A

Blues Jazz Ex. 3-A

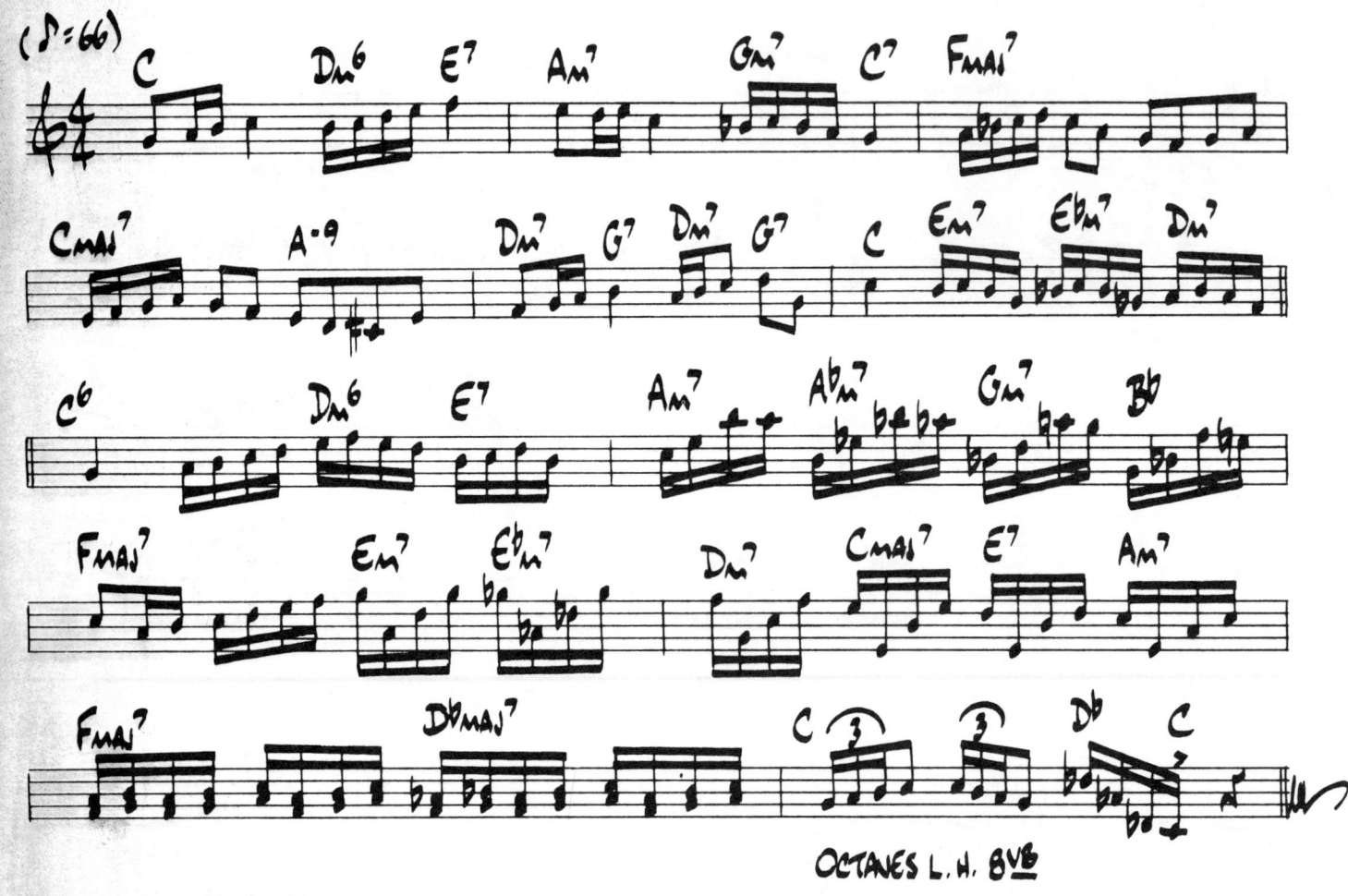

Blues Jazz Ex. 4-A

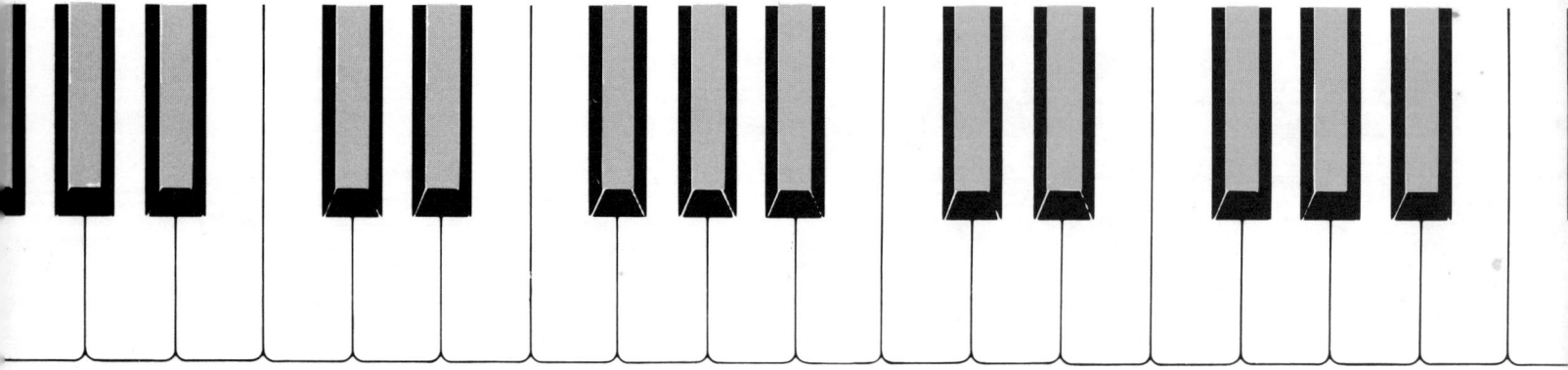

4/4 and 6/8 BLUES

The following blues choruses are played at a metronome speed of 66. The tempo remains the same throughout the piece. The 1st chorus is in 4/4 with the quarter note equal to one click. The 2nd chorus is literally double time in 6, with 2 clicks to the measure and a dotted quarter equal to one click. Then at the end, you drop back to the original feeling of reasonably slow blues.

4/4 & 6/8 Blues

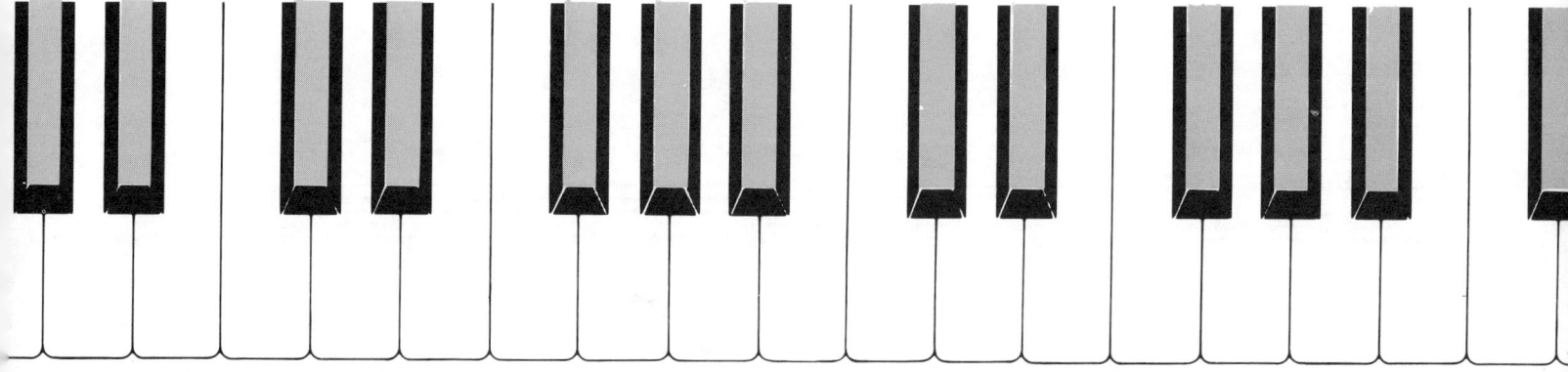

THE SIXTH WAY AND 4ths and 5ths BLUES

The following two pieces utilize the 6ths and 4ths and 5ths in place of the single note solo-type playing. On the 6th way, the figures in the right hand that are written as 4 straight 5ths should probably be played with the feeling of the 1st and 3rd notes of an 8th triplet since the tempo is reasonably slow. On the 4th and 5th blues piece, the straight 8ths should be played as is, since the tempo is up a little faster. Also note the accents on the 1st and 3rd 8th notes.

The Sixth Way

4ths & 5ths Blues

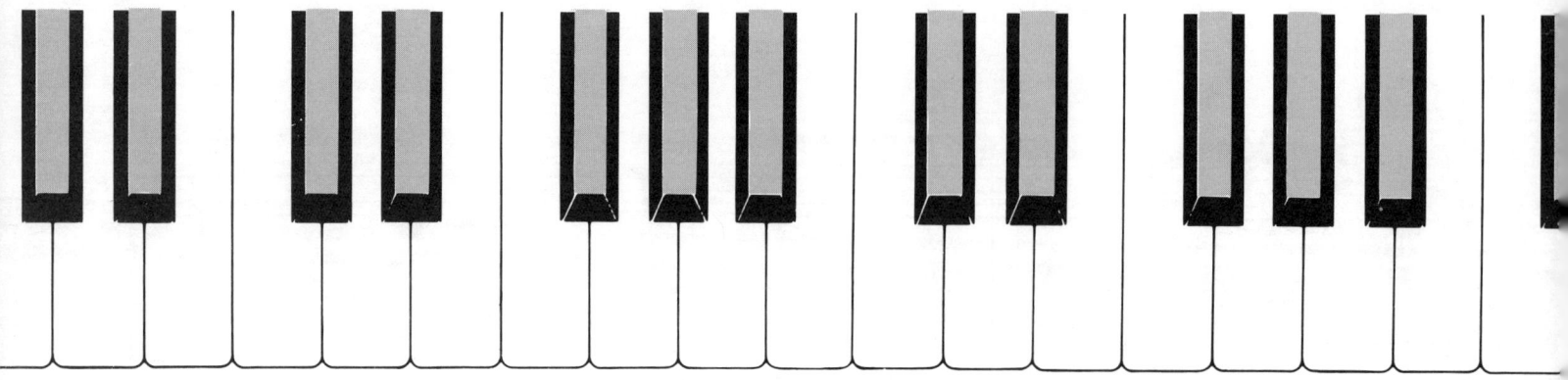

BOOGIE WOOGIE

Boogie Woogie is still basically the blues with an 8-beat bass line. There are several patterns of left-hand figures which I shall write out. The faster left-hand figures are written as straight 8ths and the slower figures are written as the 1st and 3rd notes of an 8th triplet.

I'll give a few examples of boogie woogie lines against melodies other than the blues, however I think we all agree that the boogie woogie line works best against the plain old blues.

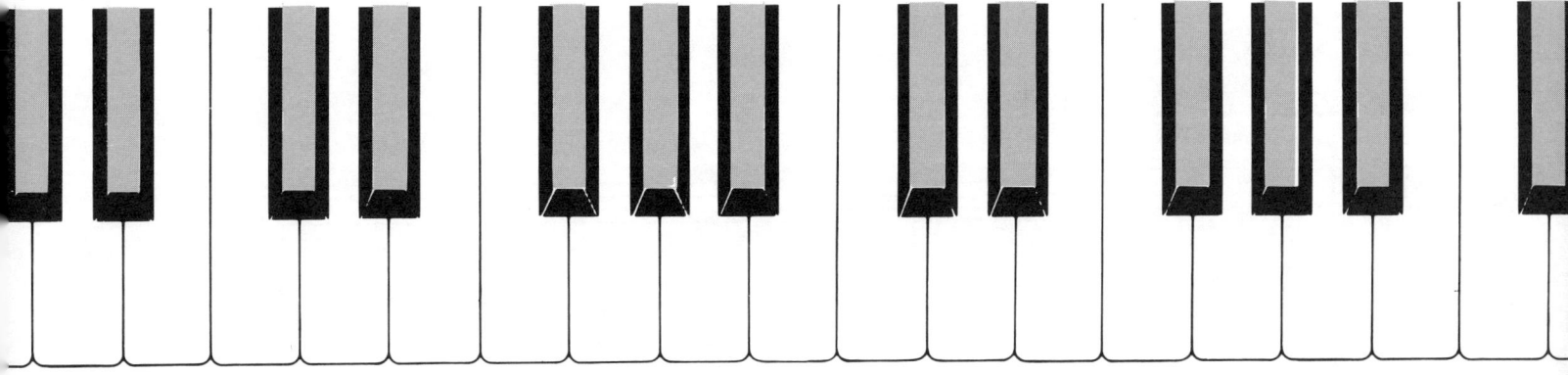

BOOGIE WOOGIE BASS LINES

The following bass lines are the 3 most common Boogie lines used. There are quite a variety of bass figures, however these are the most common so these are the ones we'll use. Again you will notice that the correct figure in the slow to medium tempo is written as the 1st and 3rd note of the 8th triplet, rather than the dotted 8th and 16th bass figure. As the tempo increases, the figures are written as straight 8ths, since the 8th triplet would give it a jerky motion which we don't need.

You must get used to playing the left hand figures automatically so you don't have to think about them when you're playing the right hand rhythms. It's a little difficult at first since this is a style of playing that hasn't been in vogue for quite a few years.

Boogie Woogie

Slow Tempo
Bass figure UP TO ♩=144

FAST TEMPO
BASS FIGURE ♩ = 144 ON UP

More Bass Figures

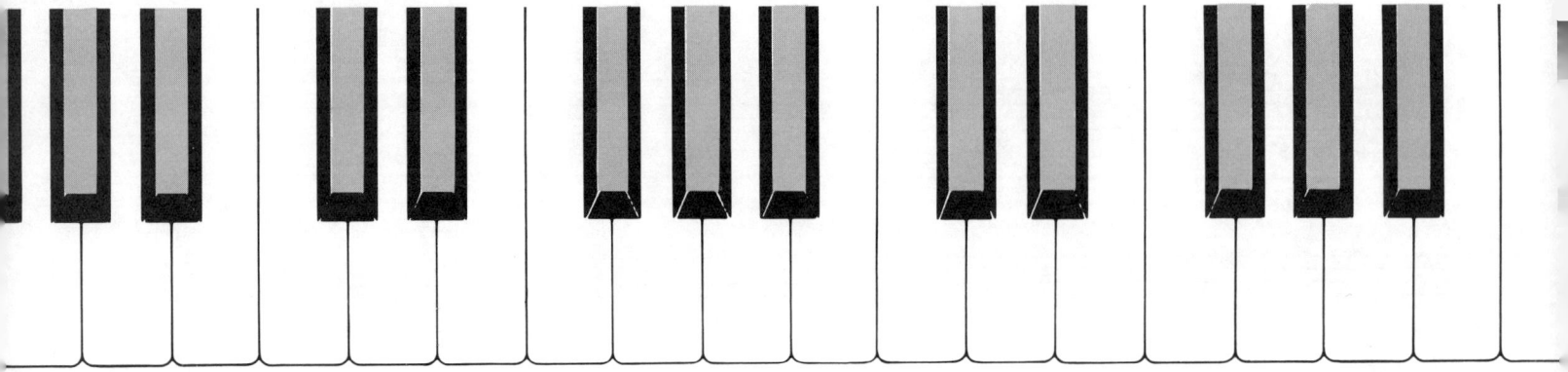

RIGHT HAND FIGURES

If the 1st right hand figure looks complicated because of the 8th triplets in the left hand and the four 16 notes in the right, think of the left hand as a dotted 8th and 16th rather than an 8th triplet and it will simplify your mental problems immediately. This will make the 1st and last notes of the left hand triplet fall on the 1st and last notes of the four 16ths. Once you get this rolling rhythm going, you are "home free."

Boogie Woogie is basically a happy type of playing, so play happily, not over-seriously. Smile when you play—show your teeth!

You may grimace occasionally in trying to put the hands together but it's well worth the effort when you get them both going.

Right Hand Figures

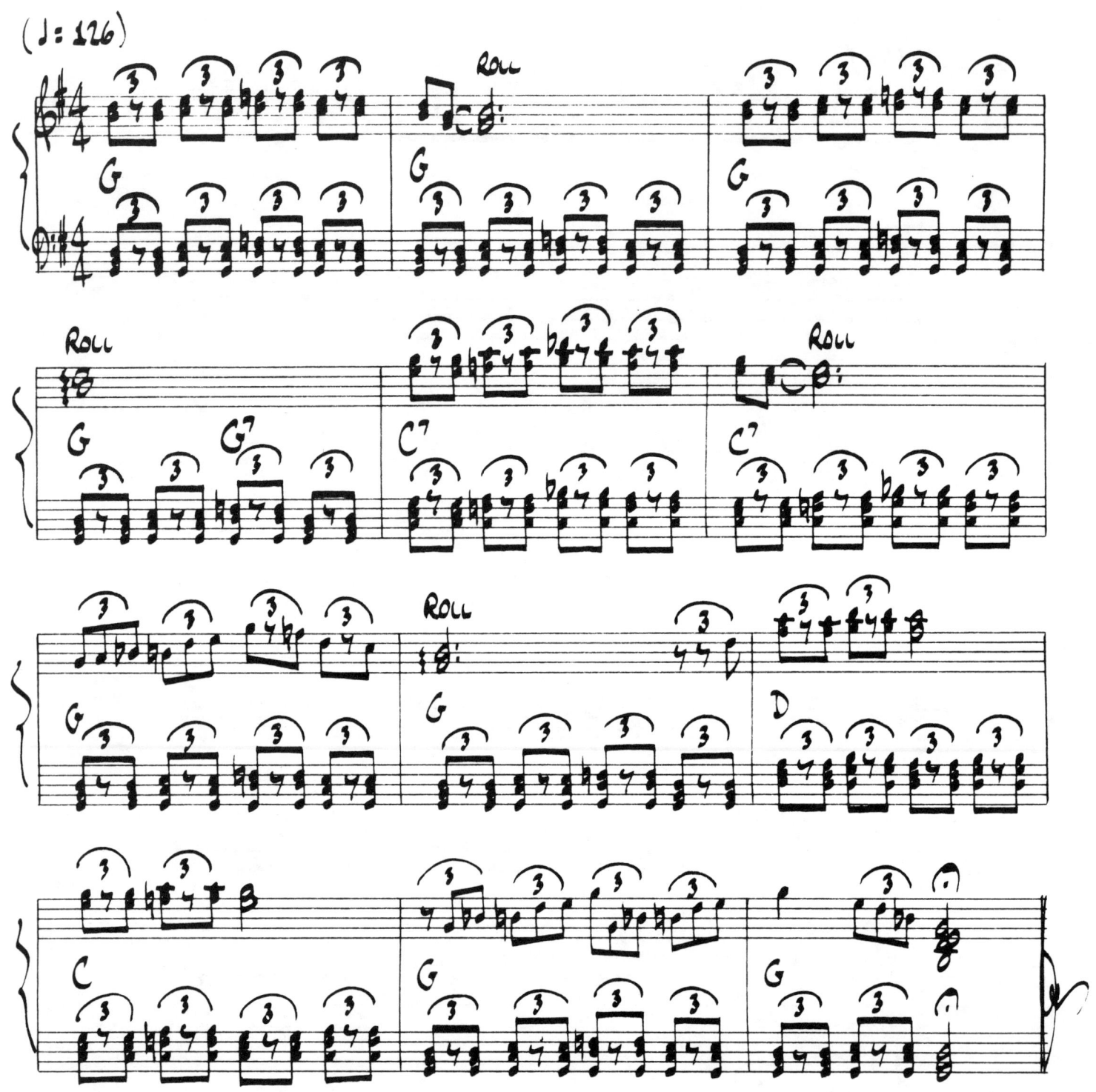

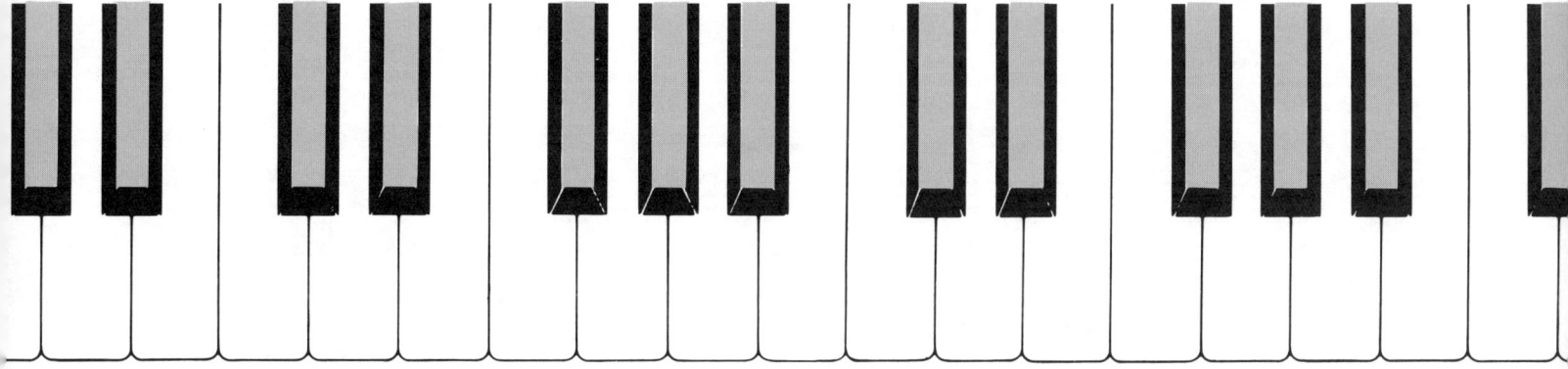

SHORT BOOGIE

This piece utilizes the 3rds and 6ths again as we did with the blues pieces earlier in the book. It will give you a few ideas to play with in place of the usual single note choruses.

Short Boogie

47

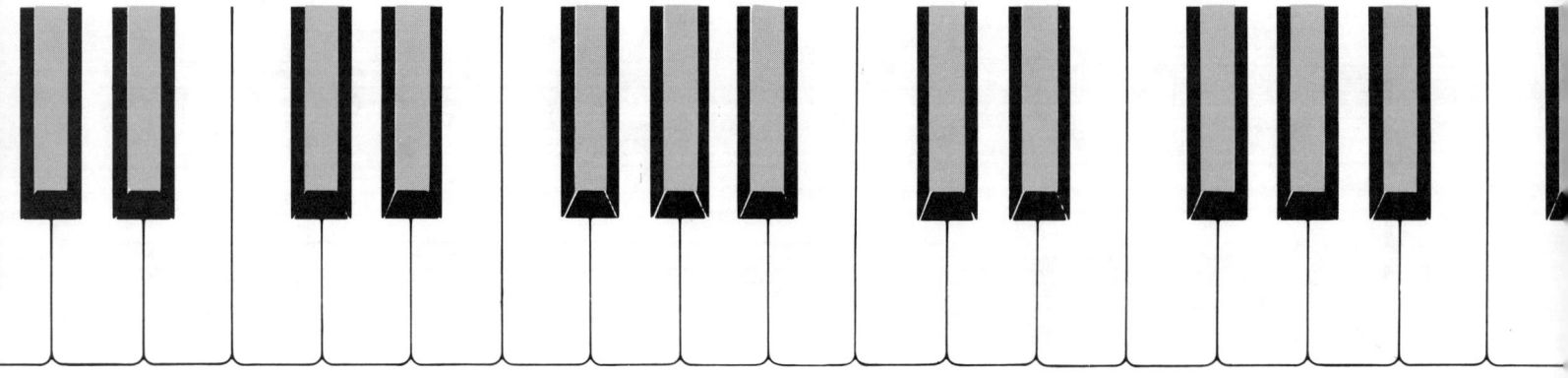

MINOR BOOGIE

You will find that playing in minor is a little more difficult than the major choruses. The left hand figures are a little more awkward to play. You have to concentrate on the bass figures a little more since they don't necessarily follow a stock pattern. The last 12 bars will be easier since they do follow more of the usual pattern.

Minor Boogie

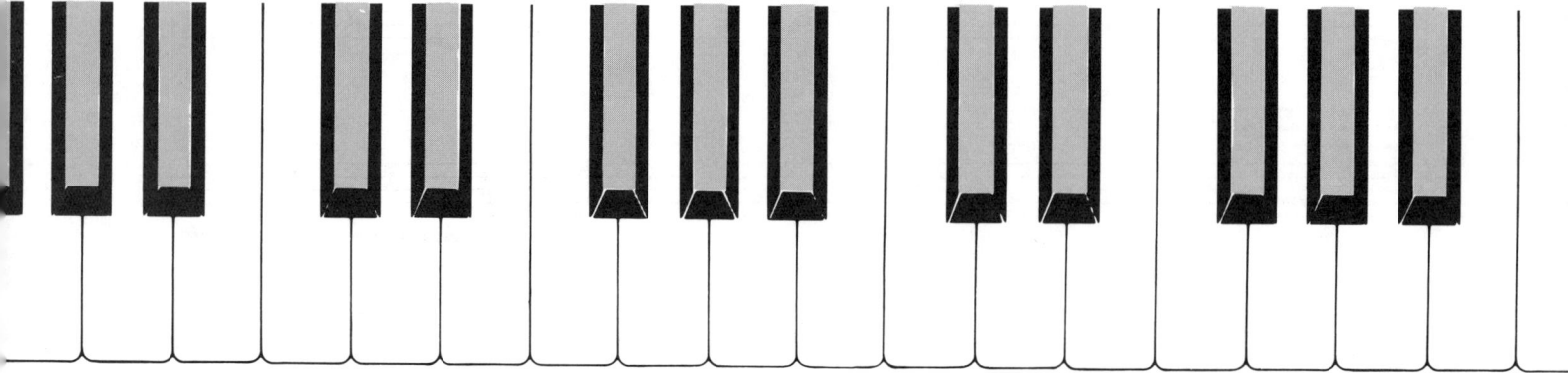

MEL'S BOOGIE

This last tune in the book is dedicated to the man who makes all these books possible. Read the right hand very carefully since it doesn't always coincide with what's going on in the left hand. Play this one with gusto!!!

Happy Boogie Boogie!!!

Paul T. Smith

Paul T. Smith

Mel's Boogie

ALSO BY THE AUTHOR

(Published by Mel Bay Publications, Inc.)

JAZZ EXERCISES FOR THE PIANO

DELUXE BLUES PIANO SOLO BOOK
(By Matt Dennis & Paul Smith)

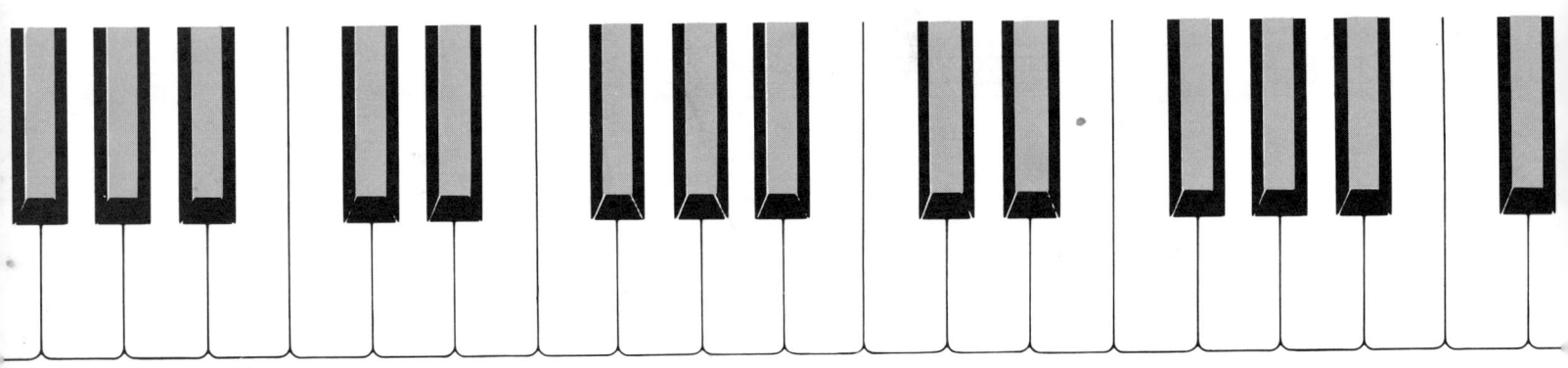

RECORDS AVAILABLE BY THE AUTHOR ON OUTSTANDING RECORDS

THE MASTER TOUCH

THE BALLAD TOUCH

THE ART TATUM TOUCH

THE ART TATUM TOUCH II

THE ALPHA TOUCH

HEAVY JAZZ I

HEAVY JAZZ II

Jazz Spotlight on Porter & Gershwin

Jazz Spotlight on Ellington and Rodgers

THIS ONE COOKS